KV-515-700

CONTENTS

Meet Poppet

This is Poppet. She lives at a Blue Cross Animal Adoption Centre. The Blue Cross is an **animal charity** that rescues and looks after unwanted and **stray** animals until they can be **rehomed**.

Many different **domestic animals** are looked after by the Blue Cross. They care for dogs, cats, goats, guinea pigs, birds and horses, as well as rabbits.

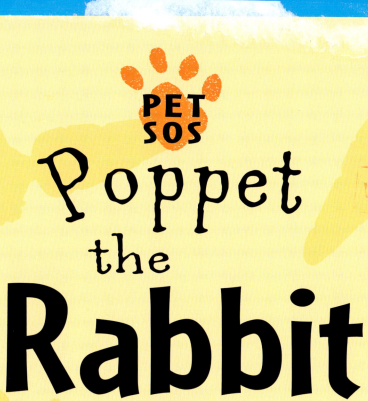

PET
SOS

Poppet
the
Rabbit

WITHDRAWN

WITHDRAWN

Tamsin Osler
Photography by Chris Fairclough

W
FRANKLIN WATTS
LONDON·SYDNEY

newcollege learning resources

238437

238437 R

NORTH EAST WORCESTERSHIRE
COLLEGE LIBRARY

636.9322 OSL

© 2001 Franklin Watts

First published in Great Britain by
Franklin Watts
96 Leonard Street
London
EC2A 4XD

Franklin Watts Australia
56 O'Riordan Street
Alexandria
NSW 2015

ISBN: 0 7496 4052 9
Dewey Decimal Classification 636.9
A CIP catalogue record for this book is available from the British Library

Printed in Malaysia

Planning and production by Discovery Books
Editors: Tamsin Osler, Kate Banham
Design: Ian Winton
Art Direction: Jason Anscomb
Photography: Chris Fairclough

Acknowledgements
The publishers would like to thank Mr and Mrs Young, their daughters
Briony and Emily, the Blue Cross and the staff at their Chalfont St Peter
Adoption Centre for their help in the production of this book.

THE BLUE CROSS
ANIMAL WELFARE CHARITY

Many animals come here because they have been abandoned. Poppet came to live here because her last owners moved house and couldn't look after her any longer.

The Blue Cross runs eleven adoption centres across the country. The Chalfont St Peter centre has staff who are experts in caring for rabbits.

The details of cats and rabbits looking for new homes are displayed on a board at the Blue Cross centre.

Life at the Blue Cross

During the warmer and drier months, the rabbits live outside in **runs**. In autumn they are brought into a special room where they are sheltered from the cold and wet.

Did you know that rabbits can be trained to use a **litter tray**? The Blue Cross tries to train all their rabbits to use litter trays. This means that only the tray, and not the whole run, has to be cleaned out daily.

Jenny is one of the centre's experts on rabbits.

Rabbits are **social animals** that need the company of other rabbits. At the Blue Cross centre, they are kept in pairs with two rabbits to a run.

The runs have fencing laid across the bottom of them to stop the rabbits digging their way out.

Each run has a hutch, with a sleeping area and a litter tray, and an outside feeding and play area with toys and tunnels.

The rabbits are fed twice a day. In the morning they are fed fresh fruit and vegetables. In the evening they are given dry food.

Jenny gives the rabbits their morning feed.

10

Dry food can be bought as a mix from most pet shops. It is important to check that it is a 'whole' food — one that contains all the **nutrients** a rabbit needs.

The rabbits must have just the right amount of food.

The rabbits are fed at the same time every evening. This helps to train them to know when to jump back into their hutch for the night.

Health check

Jenny has to make sure the rabbits are healthy. She examines the rabbits' ears regularly to make sure they are clean. There should be no liquid in them, and there shouldn't be too much wax, either.

She also checks that their eyes are clear and bright.

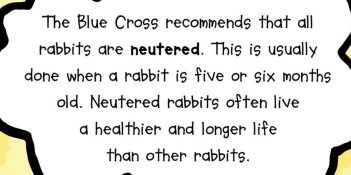

The Blue Cross recommends that all rabbits are **neutered**. This is usually done when a rabbit is five or six months old. Neutered rabbits often live a healthier and longer life than other rabbits.

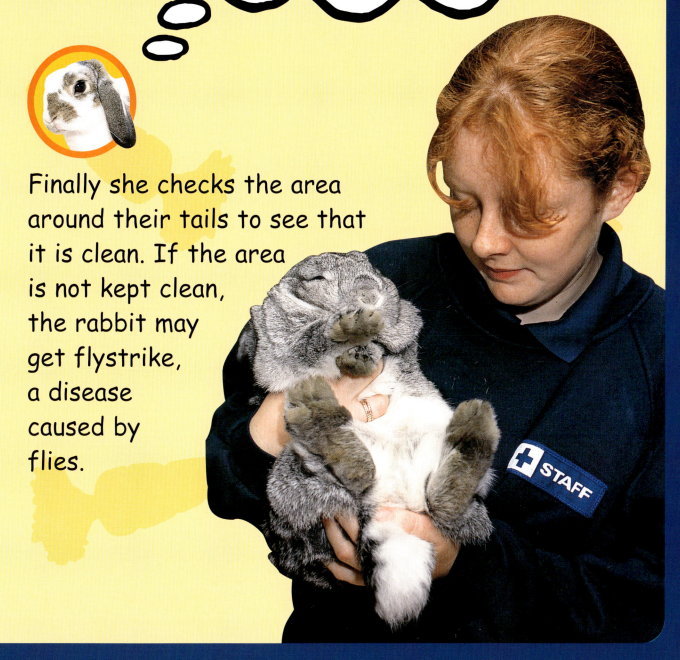

Finally she checks the area around their tails to see that it is clean. If the area is not kept clean, the rabbit may get flystrike, a disease caused by flies.

The vet

The vet visits the centre at least once a week. He checks over the new arrivals, and looks after any sick and injured animals. Some of the rabbits are overweight, so the vet has to give advice on feeding them.

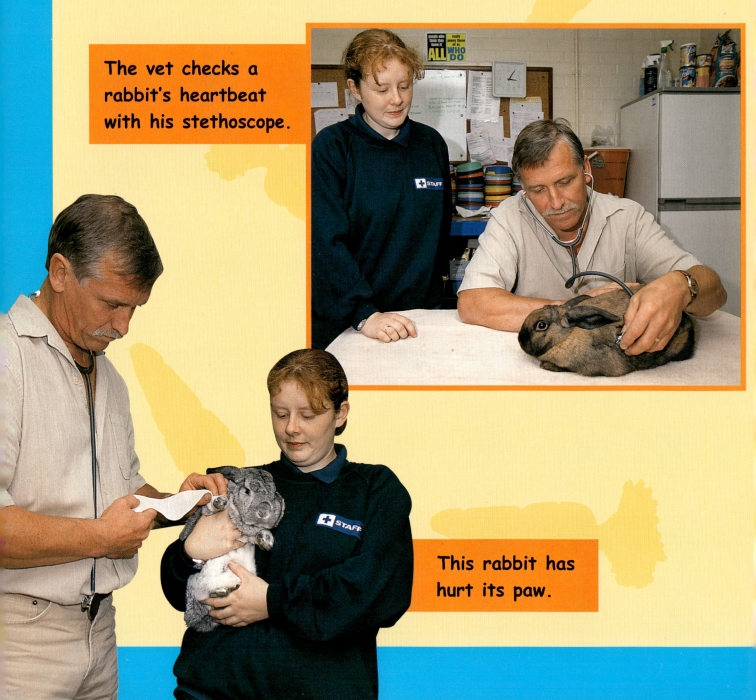

The vet checks a rabbit's heartbeat with his stethoscope.

This rabbit has hurt its paw.

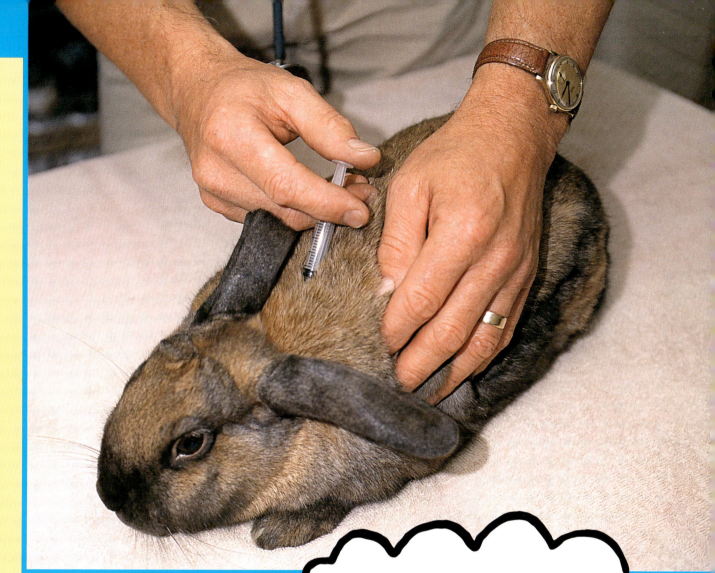

The vet also vaccinates the rabbits against a number of rabbit diseases, including myxomatosis, which has no cure.

Myxomatosis is an **infectious** rabbit disease that mainly affects wild rabbits. Domestic rabbits can catch myxomatosis if they live in an area with lots of wild rabbits.

Meet the Young family

This is the Young family. They have decided they would like to keep two rabbits, and have come to the Chalfont Adoption Centre to choose a pair.

The receptionist gives Briony and her older sister, Emily, a leaflet full of useful information about keeping rabbits.

Briony and Emily look at lots of different rabbits before they choose Poppet and Phoebe.

Rabbits can have long-haired or short-haired coats. Some have long upright ears, others have floppy ones. Floppy-eared rabbits are known as 'lops'.

Jenny shows them the rabbits in their runs, and introduces them to two female rabbits, Poppet and Phoebe, that are ready for rehoming.

Poppet is white with brown spots. Phoebe is dark chocolate brown. Both have long, floppy ears.

A new home for Poppet

Before Poppet and Phoebe can go to live with the Young family, someone from the Blue Cross visits their home to make sure it is safe for rabbits.

Emily has a special basket to bring the rabbits home in.

A few days later, the Young family return to the centre to fetch the rabbits. They fill in a form and make a donation to the centre.

Back at home, Briony and Emily let the rabbits out into their new run.

If you are thinking about keeping rabbits, try to find out as much as you can about them beforehand. The Blue Cross is a good place to go for advice.

The Blue Cross has given them lots of advice on where to place the run, and how large the hutch should be.

A rabbit's home

To live a happy and healthy life, rabbits need plenty of exercise. They need space to run around, and their hutch should be high enough for them to stand up on their hind legs.

Like the hutches at the adoption centre, Poppet and Phoebe's hutch has two areas. There is an outer area where the rabbits are fed.

The smaller inside area is where the rabbits like to sleep. Their litter tray is here too.

Rabbits are underground animals that like to dig tunnels. Briony's mother has found a large pipe that the rabbits can use as a tunnel.

Looking after rabbits

Briony and Emily look after the rabbits together.

You can give your rabbit many different vegetables and fruit including spinach, broccoli, celery, carrots, cabbage and apples. They also love dandelion leaves and clover. Make sure you wash the fruit and vegetables first.

Briony usually prepares the rabbits' food. She knows which fruit and vegetables are good for them, and which can harm them. Harmful vegetables include lettuce and raw potatoes. Poppet and Phoebe like dried rabbit food, too.

Another of Briony's tasks is to clean the hutch. She clears out the wet bedding, and spreads fresh sawdust on the hutch floor.

Briony's dad helps her to put the dirty hay and sawdust on to the compost heap.

23

One of Emily's tasks is to **groom** the rabbits. She uses a special brush to do this. Grooming helps to keep a rabbit's coat free of dirt and fleas that can make it ill.

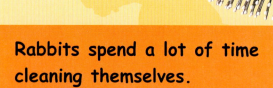

Rabbits spend a lot of time cleaning themselves.

Rabbits' teeth keep growing all the time. Poppet and Phoebe **gnaw** on hay and small branches from fruit trees to keep their teeth the right length. The girls give the rabbits fresh hay every day.

Emily checks their teeth regularly to make sure they are growing properly and are straight. She checks their ears too.

Hay helps to keep the rabbits' teeth in good condition and adds fibre to their diet.

Good times

Poppet and Phoebe have grown used to Briony and Emily, and come to them when they gently hold out a hand.

The rabbits enjoy being taken out of their run and being held too.

Briony and Emily are keeping a diary about their rabbits. They write down anything interesting they notice. Emily likes to stick in photos she has taken of them.

Looking after the rabbits is hard work at times, but both girls love it. Poppet and Phoebe have become their good friends.

The rabbits like to be wherever Briony and Emily are.

Glossary

Animal charity   An organization set up to look after animals in need.

Domestic animals   Animals that are kept as pets.

Fibre   The tough part of some plants and seeds that helps animals and people digest their food.

Gnawing   Biting and chewing, usually with the front teeth.

Groom   To brush an animal's fur or coat to remove dirt and loose hairs.

Infectious   An infectious disease is one that easily spreads or can be passed on to other animals.

Litter tray   A toilet tray for animals to use indoors.

Neutering   The operation carried out by a vet to stop animals producing young.

Nutrients   The things in food that keep you healthy and make you grow.

Parasites   Insects and animals that feed off another animal.

Rehome   To find a new home for a person or animal.

Run   A safe, enclosed area for pets to exercise and play in.

Social animals   Animals that prefer to live in groups or near other animals, rather than on their own.

Stray   An animal that has been abandoned or got lost

To vaccinate   To give medicine or treatment that protects against diseases.

Further information

The Blue Cross runs eleven adoption centres which you can visit.
To find out the addresses and opening hours of the centres local
to you, contact them on the telephone numbers below:

Bromsgrove Adoption Centre
0121 453 3130

Burford Adoption Centre
01993 822483

Cambridge Adoption Centre
01233 350153

Chalfont St Peter Adoption Centre
01753 882560

Felixstowe Adoption Centre
01394 283254

Hertfordshire Adoption Centre
01438 832232

Northiam Equine & Adoption Centre
01797 252243

Southampton Adoption Centre
023 8069 2894

Thirsk Adoption Centre
01845 577759

Tiverton Adoption Centre
01884 855291

Torbay Adoption Centre
01803 327728

Other organizations to contact include
the Royal Society for the Prevention
of Cruelty to Animals (RSPCA) and the
British House Rabbit Association:

RSPCA
Causeway, Horsham, West Sussex
RH12 1HG
Tel: 01403 264181

The British House Rabbit Association
PO Box 346, Newcastle upon Tyne
NE99 1FA

In Australia you can contact:
House Rabbit Association of Australia
PO Box 30
Riverton, WA 6148

Rabbit Information Service
Tel: (08) 9354 2985
rabbit@iinet.net.au

Australian Animal Protection Society
10 Homeleigh Road
Keysborough, VIC 3173
Email: enquiries@aaps.org.au

RSPCA Australia
201 Rookwood Road
Yagoona, NSW 2199
Tel: (02) 9709 5433
www.rspca.org.au

Index